VENICE THE CITY BY NIGHT

LUCA CAMPIGOTTO

VENICE THE CITY BY NIGHT

Frontispiece:
LIDO, SAN NICOLETTO, 1992

Translated from the Italian *Venezia immaginario notturno*

Editing: Alessandra Mauro
Book Design: Hugo de Carvalho junior
Layout: Angelo Rinna

First published in the United Kingdom in 2006 by
Thames & Hudson Ltd, 181A High Holborn, London WC1V 7QX

www.thamesandhudson.com

Photographs © 2006 Luca Campigotto
Texts © 2006 the authors
The essay 'Venice' by Henry James was first published
in *The Century Magazine*, XXV (November 1882).

Original edition © 2006 Contrasto, Rome
This edition © 2006 Thames & Hudson Ltd, London

British Library Cataloguing-in-Publication Data
A catalogue record for this book is available from the British Library

ISBN-10: 0-500-54318-6
ISBN-13: 978-0-500-54318-4

Printed and bound in Italy

CONTENTS

VENICE

HENRY JAMES

It is a great pleasure to write the word; but I am not sure there is not a certain impudence in pretending to add anything to it. Venice has been painted and described many thousands of times, and of all the cities of the world is the easiest to visit without going there. Open the first book and you will find a rhapsody about it; step into the first picture-dealer's and you will find three or four high-coloured 'views' of it. There is notoriously nothing more to be said on the subject. Every one has been there, and every one has brought back a collection of photographs. There is as little mystery about the Grand Canal as about our local thoroughfare, and the name of St Mark is as familiar as the postman's ring. It is not forbidden, however, to speak of familiar things, and I hold that for the true Venice-lover Venice is always in order. There is nothing new to be said about her certainly, but the old is better than any novelty. It would be a sad day indeed when there should be something new to say. I write these lines with the full conscious-ness of having no information whatever to offer. I do not pretend to enlighten the reader; I pretend only to give a fil-lip to his memory; and I hold any writer sufficiently justified who is himself in love with his theme....

II

The danger is that you will not linger enough - a danger of which the author of these lines had known something. It is possible to dislike Venice, and to entertain the sentiment in a responsible and intelligent manner. There are trav-ellers who think the place odious, and those who are not of this opinion often find themselves wishing that the others were only more numerous. The sentimental tourist's sole quarrel with his Venice is that he has too many competi-tors there. He likes to be alone; to be original; to have (to himself, at least) the air of making discoveries. The Venice of to-day is a vast museum where the little wicket that admits you is perpetually turning and creaking, and you march through the institution with a herd of fellow-gazers. There is nothing left to discover or describe and originality of attitude is completely impossible. This is often very annoying; you can only turn your back on your impertinent playfellow and curse his want of delicacy. But this is not the fault of Venice; it is the fault of the rest of the world. The fault of Venice is that, though she is easy to admire, she is not so easy to live with as you count living in other places. After you have stayed a week and the bloom of novelty has rubbed off you wonder if you can accommo-date yourself to the peculiar conditions. Your old habits become impracticable and you find yourself obliged to form new ones of an undesirable and unprofitable charac-ter. You are tired of your gondola (or you think you are) and you have seen all the principal pictures and heard the names of the palaces announced a dozen times by your gondolier, who brings them out almost as impressively as if he were an English butler bawling titles into a drawing-room. You have walked several hundred times round the Piazza and bought several bushels of photographs. You have visited the antiquity mongers whose horrible sign-boards dishonour some of the grandest vistas in the Grand Canal; you have tried the opera and found it very bad; you have bathed at the Lido and found the water flat. You have begun to have a shipboard-feeling – to regard the Piazza as an enormous saloon and the Riva degli Schiavoni as a promenade-deck. You are obstructed and encaged; your desire for space is unsatisfied; you miss your usual exercise. You try to take a walk and you fail, and meantime, as I say, you have come to regard your gondola as a sort of magnified baby's cradle. You have no desire to be rocked to sleep, though you are sufficiently kept awake by the irritation produced, as you gaze across the shallow lagoon, by the attitude of the perpetual gondolier, with his turned-out toes, his protruded chin, his absurdly unscientific stroke.

The canals have a horrible smell, and the everlasting Piazza, where you have looked repeatedly at every article in every shop-window and found them all rubbish, where the young Venetians who sell bead bracelets and 'panoramas' are perpetually thrusting their wares at you, where the same tightly-buttoned officers are for ever sucking the same black weeds, at the same empty tables, in front of the same cafés – the Piazza, as I say, has resolved itself into a magnificent tread-mill. This is the state of mind of those shallow inquirers who find Venice all very well for a week; and if in such a state of mind you take your departure you act with fatal rashness. The loss is your own,

moreover; it is not – with all deference to your personal attractions – that of your companions who remain behind; for though there are some disagreeable things in Venice there is nothing so disagreeable as the visitors. The conditions are peculiar, but your intolerance of them evaporates before it has had time to become a prejudice. When you have called for the bill to go, pay it and remain, and you will find on the morrow that you are deeply attached to Venice. It is by living there from day to day that you feel the fulness of her charm; that you invite her exquisite influence to sink into your spirit. The creature varies like a nervous woman, whom you know only when you know all the aspects of her beauty. She has high spirits or low, she is pale or red, grey or pink, cold or warm, fresh or wan, according to the weather or the hour. She is always interesting and almost always sad; but she has a thousand occasional graces and is always liable to happy accidents. You become extraordinarily fond of these things, you count upon them; they make part of your life. Tenderly fond you become; there is something indefinable in those depths of personal acquaintance that gradually establish themselves. The place seems to personify itself, to become human and sentient and conscious of your affection. You desire to embrace it, to caress it, to possess it; and finally a soft sense of possession grows up and your visit becomes a perpetual love-affair.

Originally published in *The Century Magazine*, XXV (November 1882)

A TIMELESS PLACE

LUCA CAMPIGOTTO

It was the winter of 1991, and I was a photographer in search of inspiration. In the absence of a vast frontier to explore (in my heart, Robert Adams's Wild West, Roger Fenton's Crimean battlefields, or the Beato brothers' Cairo), I went out one evening with a reflex camera and attempted to take my first nocturnal photos of Venice. It was very dark and cold; I clicked the shutter just a few times, thinking that nothing would come out, and hurried back home.

It came as a surprise, the following day, when I discovered that the images I had shot conjured up a theatrical atmosphere. In the semi-transparency of the negatives, there also seemed to be a sense of humidity; the familiar sound of the water, which scarcely moves. So I borrowed a plate camera – a sole point of contact with my favourite artists – and began to systematically photograph the city.

While I was waiting for the long exposures, I wondered whether it had been a good idea to choose such a difficult subject. As a student of history, I had grown accustomed to telling the tale of Venice through the unquestionable content of archived documents and the reconstructions in great history books. But now, for the first time, I was looking at the place where I lived with the care of someone wanting to express a personal viewpoint. I was aware that the beauty of the place – its evident poetic quality – was stronger than any rhetoric. But the endless iconography that exists made it impossible to attempt a fresh approach – a renewed innocence in the way I viewed it. 'The anxiety of capturing a landscape that can do without me', as Joseph Brodsky wrote, came to me in the enchantment of the deserted streets.

Finally, because of my bond, I took a gamble, using as my reference the obsessive love demonstrated by the great photographers – Eugène Atget, lost in the streets of Paris; Bernardo Bellotto, who revisited Dresden again and again.

As I took one step after another, my clear awareness of the crumbling walls and canals mingled with the golden age of La Serenissima, which I had inherited from books. The scene recalled nights of long ago that I had never known.

The most humid night of the summer, sleepless and stifling, just as it was before the onset of the plague. The city emptied of its citizens, barricaded to ward off the disease. The night when the Consiglio dei Dieci gathered for a dramatic emergency council, while the sirocco raged under the porticos and the water seeped into every crevice. Or the night when the explosions and fires of the Turks ripped through the darkness, with the sinister, whirling flicker of the aft lanterns further afield, the brusque dance of the ships turning in battle.

But also many centuries of nights that unfolded without anything extraordinary coming to pass. Nights in the open air, amid the cries and coughs that rose to the palazzo windows from the jetty, crowded with fires and sails. Nights soaked in the odour of stacked Polish wood - swollen with water like corpses - beyond the walls of the Arsenale. Nights scarred by the ominous dreams of the many who, over the course of the centuries, left this place never to return. Nights of hasty decisions that changed entire lives and always seemed to come down to a matter of the Orient, a journey or an ex-lover.

And then the patrol of the 'Signori di Notte'. The hunt for libertines fleeing through the lagoon. The moonlight shining on the gamblers. The relentless sneering of the courtesans from an illuminated balcony. The feverish work of the merchants, bent over their accounts by candlelight, eager to get to the young serving wench in the attic.

Through the photographic surface - with its ambiguous, inevitably deceptive nature - I have tried to rebuild these scenes in my imagination.

Venice is an ancient widow. Every night sickly and sublime, when she is left to herself, to the cats, to her band of rejected lovers. In the dark, her body lets itself be explored; an archive that reveals the very archaeology of the landscape, and allows us the privilege of travelling back in time.

The photographs bring the unforgettable to life. I love them because they give the illusion that we may find once again the things we have lost, or that we never possessed. A last glance can take the thing that we fear we may never see again and transform it into an icon. In the persuasive unfaithfulness of black and white, the dream is premeditated. Photography may well be nostalgia's greatest tool.

The trade of the night,

watching over the lights

of a film set

not long deserted.

The backdrop on which its destiny

will belatedly appear.

The theatres of insomnia, woven

from the swarming of the pursuers.

Where in the insidious shadows,

it is easy to see yourself as the watchman

on your hands and knees, looking out

over the enemy camp.

Or the archaeologist,

who lightly dusts

the backbone of a city

exhumed. Always love,

origins, ink. A panther

who stops baring her teeth

and lets herself be stroked.

L. C.

CAMPO SANTA MARIA FORMOSA, 1991

COVERED PASSAGEWAY OUTSIDE THE PRISON, 1993

RIALTO BRIDGE, 1992

RIALTO, 1991

PAGES 20-21 GRAND CANAL, ACCADEMIA, 1991

GRAND CANAL, SCALZI, 1991

RIALTO, CANAL BEND, 1991

PAGE 26 RIALTO, 1992
PAGE 27 GRAND CANAL, SAN STAE, 1991

RIO DEI MENDICANTI, 1992

MARCO POLO'S HOUSE, RIO DE SAN LIO, 1991

SAN FRANCESCO DE LA VIGNA, 1992

PAGE 34 GHETTO NOVO, 1991
PAGE 35 RIO DE SANTA MARINA 1, 1991
PAGES 36-37 RIO DE SANTA MARINA 2, 1991

BRIDGE OF SIGHS, 1993

RIO DE LA CANONICA, 1993

PAGE 42 RIO DE VERONA, 1992
PAGE 43 PONTE DE LA CANONICA, 1992

RIO DE SANTA MARIA ZOBENIGO, 1992

CAMPO SANTA MARIA FORMOSA, 1991

RIO DE SAN MARCUOLA, 1992

PAGES 58-59 GRAND CANAL, FONTEGO DEI TURCHI, 1991

CA' PESARO, 1999

RIALTO, PESCARIA, 1992

RIO DE SAN SEVERO, 1993

PIAZZA SAN MARCO, HIGH WATER, 1992

PAGES 68, 69 PIAZZA SAN MARCO, HIGH WATER AT THE PROCURATIE VECCHIE, 1992

PORTICO IN THE DOGE'S PALACE, HIGH WATER, 1992

FONDAMENTA ZATTERE, MAGAZZINI DEL SALE, 1992

PAGES 74-75 CANALE DE LA GIUDECCA, SANT'EUFEMIA, 1991

GIUDECCA, RIO DE LA CROCE, 1991

PAGES 78, 79 ARSENALE DOCKYARD, GAGGIANDRE, 1999
PAGES 80-81 GIUDECCA, 1992

SANT'ALVISE, 1992

PAGE 84 MOLINO STUCKY, 1992
PAGE 85 ARSENALE DOCKYARD, 1992

ARSENALE DOCKYARD, 1992

LIDO, MALAMOCCO, 1992

90-91 MARGHERA, 1992

MARGHERA, LAST NIGHT

LUCA CAMPIGOTTO

It was pitch-black and the windscreen wiper was smearing the dirt up and down the glass. I was leaning forward as I drove, zigzagging my way between the puddles, with the headlights darting here and there as if looking for a fugitive in the undergrowth. A slow song was playing on the radio, almost drowned out by the sound of the fan heater. The mobile phone on the passenger seat lay silent. 'Madame' was unlikely to call back. She was a night-owl but it was too late even for her. Another missed chance to have a drink with her, I thought to myself, convinced that she would have liked to explore those mysterious places.

Personally, I love industrial areas: they are my patch; I feel at home there. The cracked asphalt that gleams in the light, rising up to form a crust when it crosses the rail tracks. The tall outlines of the towers and bridges, blacker than the sky outside the window. The cranes that rise up like the necks of dinosaurs from behind the illuminated smoke. The strange lights: too bright or almost impossible to see, dying out the further they get from the city walls. And then the electronic gates, and the cabins of the night-watchmen. And, every now and then, a parked car here or there: lovers hiding between stacks of pipes and deserted train carriages.

Once again, on that night it seemed that everything had been arranged there like a stage set. By the gangways of the ships, the yellow lights framed the low, round fuel tanks. The grass was coated in a layer of grease and a transparent mist rose from the reeking water.

Suddenly I felt more tired than usual. I pulled over and turned off the headlights and the radio. I put back the seat and dozed off. In my dream I had a left-luggage ticket in my pocket, and I was standing still on a platform, waiting for an assassin with a deformed face to turn up with a hostage at gunpoint. A suitcase full of cash, in exchange for 'Madame', who was huddled up, frozen. That night was to become the central scene of our story. The moment when there should have appeared on set a Chinese gangster in a blue, double-breasted jacket, a hat and dark glasses. A blonde, a little shaken, with rope marks on her wrists, and swollen eyes full of melancholy irony. And Marlowe standing right in front of them, impassable, with Bogart's sneer on his lips....

VIA DELLE INDUSTRIE, 1996

BANCHINA DEI MOLINI 1, 1996

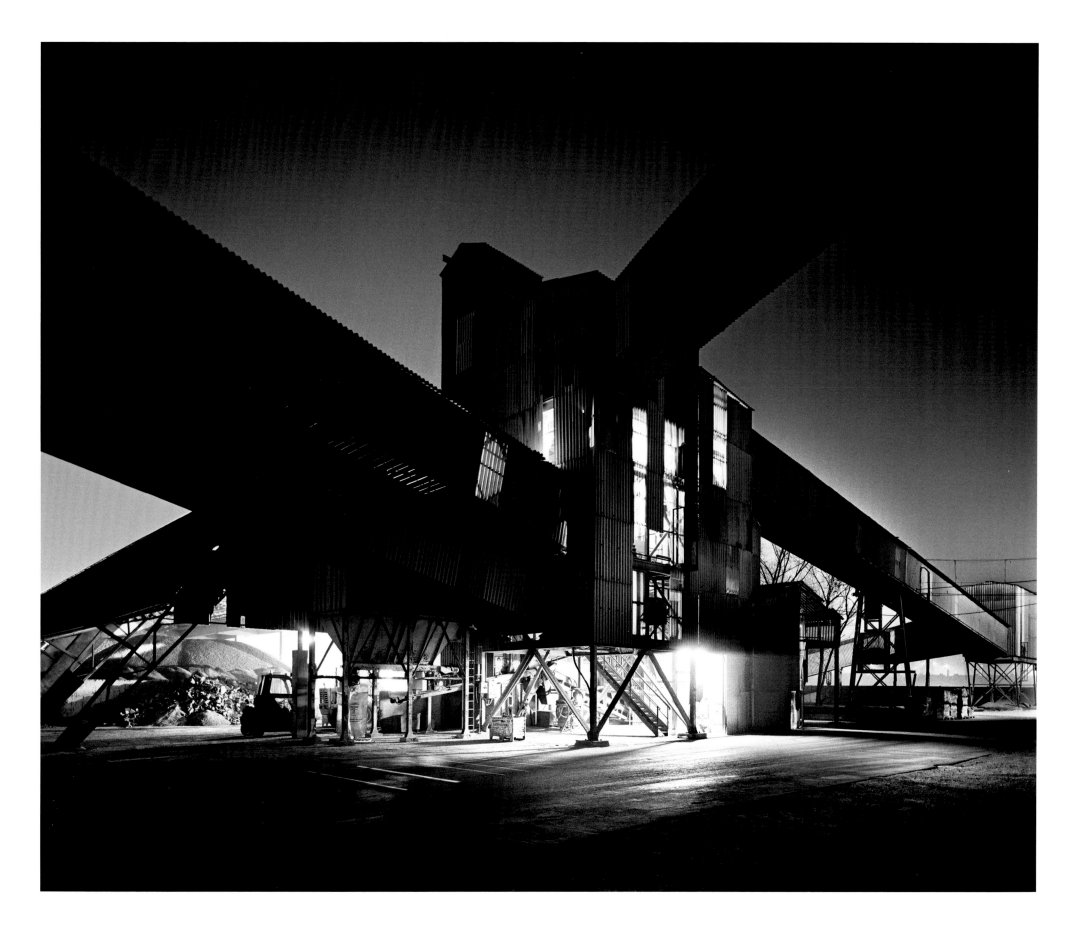

BANCHINA CANALE INDUSTRIALE NORD 1, 1996

FINCANTIERI SHIPYARD 3, 1997

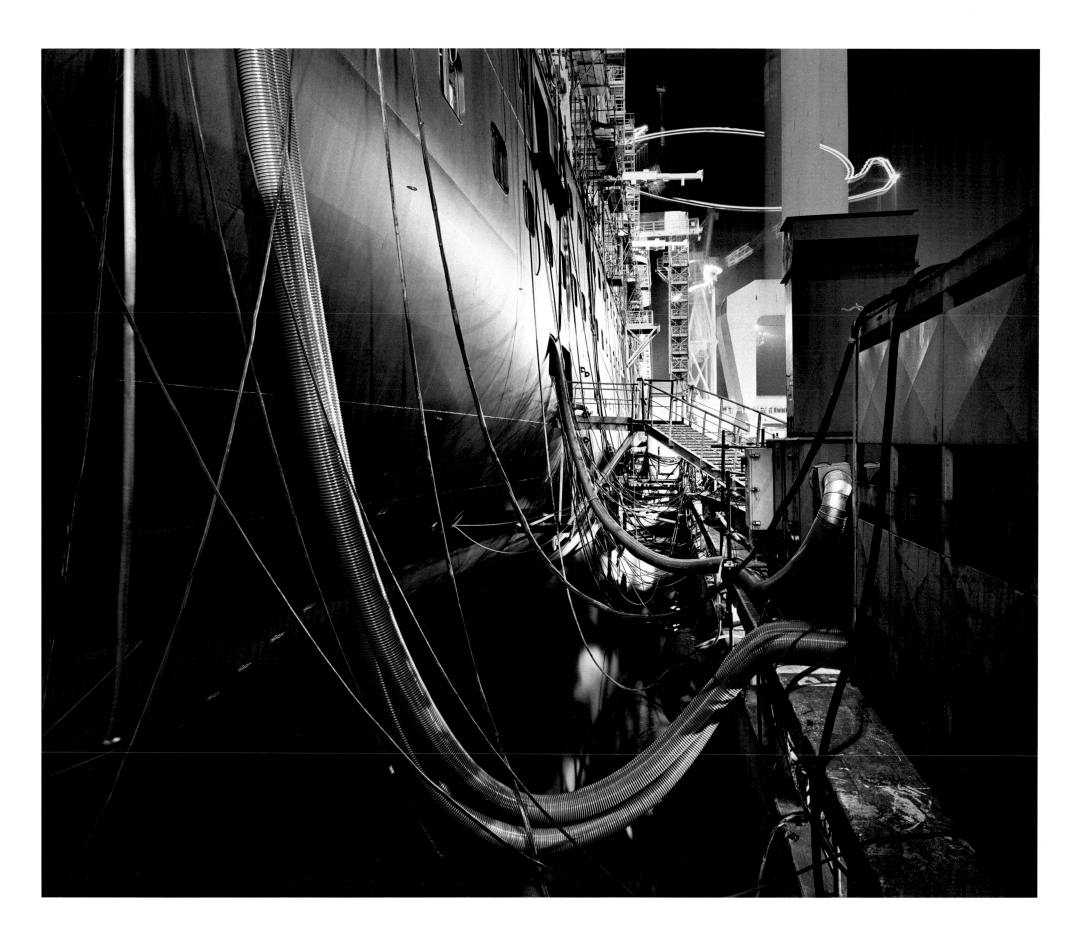

PAGE 108 FINCANTIERI SHIPYARD 4, 1997
PAGE 109 FINCANTIERI SHIPYARD 5, 1997

FINCANTIERI SHIPYARD 6, 1997

FINCANTIERI SHIPYARD 7, 1997

BANCHINA DEI MOLINI 3, 1996

CANALE INDUSTRIALE, 1996

Luca Campigotto was born in Venice in 1962. He has a degree in modern history and began to take photographs in the early 1980s, focusing on his own passion for landscape, architecture and industry. From 1990 onwards, his personal projects have been interspersed with a range of commissions that have taken him to Venice, Rome, Naples, New York, Chicago, Cairo, Morocco and Patagonia.

He has taken part in group exhibitions that include: Mois de la Photo, Paris; 47' Venice Biennale; MAXXI, Rome; MEP, Paris; IVAM, Valencia; Galleria Gottardo, Lugano; The Art Museum, Florida; CCA, Montreal.

Among the public and private collections that feature his work are the Maison Européenne de la Photographie, Paris; Canadian Centre for Architecture, Montreal; Progressive Art Collection, Cleveland; Margulies Collection, Miami; Sagamore, Miami; Collezione Unicredit, Milan; Fondazione Sandretto Re Rebaudengo, Turin; Museo Fortuny, Venice; Museo d'Arte Moderna e Contemporanea, Varese; Galleria Civica, Modena; Museo della Fotografia, Cinisello Balsamo; Museo Civico, Riva del Garda; CRAF, Spilimbergo.

His published work includes: *Sguardi gardesani*, 2004; *L'Arsenale di Venezia*, 2000; *Fuori di casa*, 1998; *Molino Stucky*, 1998; *Venetia Obscura*, 1995. He is also interested in writing, and in 2005 the magazine *Nuovi Argomenti* published a selection of his photographs and poetry.

www.lucacampigotto.com